CODES

to connect you with

SOURCE

ISBN 978-0-6453603-0-1

Author | Designer | Publication by

Elida Stevans

channel.elidastevans.com.au

Throughout time and space the All chooses to experience complete separation only to rediscover that it was always fully and completely within the All.

The codes within these words reflect the essence of self within the All, as the All experiences itself in individual ways within the One who is having the experience.

The words require reflection in order for the meaning to be fully received by the individual through one's own divine experience of the All.

I Am AS ONE

WITH THE *All*

AS THE *All*

IS *One* WITH

THE *Am*

THAT *I Am*

I Am

IMMORTAL

I Am

EVERLASTING

I Am

A SEED OF *light*

I Am

A SEED OF *love*

WHEN MY INNER *light*

WARMS THE SEED

OF INNER *love*

FRUIT WILL BE PRODUCED

THAT WILL BE BOUNTIFUL AND

BLESSED

FOR ALL WITHIN MY PRESENCE

I FORGIVE ALL

WHEN *I love* THE

Am

THAT *I Am*

DIVISION

IS A REALM OF THE EYES

ESSENCE

KNOWS NO DIVISION

I HEAL

WHEN *I love* FULLY

all

THAT *I Am*

all

THAT *I* HAVE BEEN AND

all

THAT *I* DESIRE TO BE

JUDGMENT

HAS NO ROOTS

WHEN THE HEART IS FILLED

WITH *love*

THERE IS NO

EXTERNAL

ONLY A MIRROR OF THE

INTERNAL

THE SEED OF *light* WITHIN

REQUIRES

DAILY ATTENTION

THE SEED OF *light* WITHIN

DESIRES TO BLOOM

AND

TO BE FRUITFUL

THE SEED OF *light* WITHIN

CARES FOR LIFE

INCLUDING THE BODY

OF THE GREAT DIVINE MOTHER

THE SEED OF *light* WITHIN

CARES TO GIVE

AND IN THE GIVING

RECEIVES PLEASURE

OF ITS OWN GROWTH AND

EXPANSION

BEYOND ITSELF

BEYOND ITS IMMEDIATE FAMILY

BEYOND ITS

PLANETARY CONSCIOUSNESS

THE SEED OF *love* WITHIN

SEEKS FERTILE

SOIL

ONLY THROUGH GIVING

OF ITSELF

WITHOUT JUDGMENT

WITHOUT FEAR

WITHOUT PREJUDICE

THE SEED OF *love* WITHIN

UNDERSTANDS

THAT *All*

IS *One*

AS *One* IS WITHIN

THE *All*

THERE IS NO POWER GREATER

THAN THE INTERNAL UNION

BETWEEN

THE SEED OF *light*

AND THE SEED OF *love*

YOUR *will*

IS THE AVENUE

THAT ALLOWS THE TWO SEEDS

TO UNITE

YOUR *will* TO BE

IN HONOUR OF

YOUR CURRENT EXPRESSION OF

SELF

YOUR *will* TO SEE

THAT OTHERS ARE

NO DIFFERENT TO YOU

AND SEEK WHAT YOU SEEK

YOU ARE FREE

TO YIELD YOUR *will*

TO GENERATE *love*

UNTO YOUR SEEDS

COMPASSION

UNTO YOURSELF AND

RECOGNITION

OF THE DIVINE FORCE

PROPELLING YOU

TO AWAKEN

TO THE INTERNAL TRUTH

OF YOUR PRESENT EXISTENCE

ALWAYS PRESENT

ALWAYS PRESENT

WITHIN YOUR PRESENT

YOUR SEED OF *light*

AND YOUR SEED OF *love*

BECOME ENERGISED

WITHIN YOUR PRESENT

YOU ARE THE *All*

WITHIN THE *One*

WITHIN YOUR PRESENT

THE *One* IS WITHIN

THE *All*

BE PRESENT

BE ALWAYS PRESENT

THE PRESENT

REVEALS WHAT IS NEEDED

THE PRESENT

IS THE *All*

COMMUNICATING TO YOU

THE *All*

IS A MOMENT OF INFINITY

EVERPRESENT

SEEK TO BE

EVER

PRESENT

DIRECT YOUR *will*

TO THE INTERNAL

SEED OF *light*

AND THE INTERNAL

SEED OF *love*

ENERGISE

THESE SEEDS

AND AS THEY UNITE

YOU WILL BEAR THE FRUITS

OF

DIVINE CREATION

YOU WILL BE

IN DIVINE UNION

WITH THE *All*

THAT IS

WITHIN THE *One*

AS THE

I Am IS ALWAYS

WITHIN THE *All*

BE AS *One*

WITH THE *All*

AND THE *All*

WILL DWELL

WITHIN THE *I Am*

IN BLESSED WAYS

AND IN DIVINE UNIONS

www.ingramcontent.com/pod-product-compliance
Lightning Source LLC
Chambersburg PA
CBHW041823090426
42811CB00010B/1087